MW01113744

Pass The Salt Please!
Seasoned Believers Add Flavor To Your Life
By
Brenda Diann Johnson

Aswiftt Publishing, LLC
Duncanville, Texas 75138
www.aswifttpublishing.com
Book Cover Design by
Brenda Diann Johnson

Brenda Diann Johnson
E-mail: brendadiannjohnson@yahoo.com

Published by
Aswiftt Publishing, LLC
P.O. Box 380669
Duncanville, Texas 75138-0669

ISBN: 978-0-9910816-0-8

Library of Congress Control Number: 2014904413

Printed in the United States of America

All scripture quotations are from the King James Version of
the Bible unless otherwise noted. All definitions are from The
Random House College Dictionary, Revised Ed. unless
otherwise noted.

Cover Design and Editing by Brenda Diann Johnson

Dedications

I dedicate *Pass The Salt Please! Seasoned Believers Add Flavor To Your Life* to My Mother, Thelma Byrd Robinson, who taught me that prayer was a necessity for my life. I remember as a child seeing my mom petitioning God during some tough times. My Aunt, Rosie Willis, who continues to be a co-parent to me and my children. She has been there for us unconditionally.

Mary Stephens, who treated me like her own daughter when I married her son Billy. She still considers me as family after the passing of her son. My spiritual mothers and fathers, who mentored, taught and encouraged me. Your wealth of knowledge has been a benefit over the years to me.

Lastly, I thank God for prayer partners and other mentors He brought into my life to teach, encourage and propel me to spiritual growth.

Acknowledgments

I give due respect to the ministries that helped me to grow to spiritual maturity over the years.

St. Stephens Baptist Church in Wharton, Texas.

The Church of the Nazarines in Dallas, Texas

Tabernacle Missionary Baptist Church in Dallas, Texas

Oak Cliff Bible Fellowship in Dallas, Texas

Rising Star Missionary Baptist Church in Fort Worth, Texas

The Potter's House in Dallas, Texas

Prestonwood Baptist Church in Plano, Texas

Table of Contents

Introduction

Introduction

Pass The Salt Please! Seasoned Believers Add Flavor To Your Life is a reference guide to aid and propel new Christians to spiritual growth. This book will help young believers and babes in Christ stay on track with their destiny. Young believers may often miss the mark in what God has commanded them to do. When you miss the mark don't be discouraged. Repent and ask God for forgiveness. Get back up and continue to strive everyday toward spiritual maturity.

When new converts repent and turn away from a life of sin, accept Jesus Christ as their Lord and Savior and decide to live according to God's word, they will need mentoring, prayer and support on their new journey.

It is important for new Christians to become a part of a local church where they can serve, learn about God's word and grow to spiritual maturity. New Christians should have a network of Seasoned Believers who support, mentor and pray for them.

Studying the word of God is an ongoing responsibility for all Christians. According to 2 Timothy 2:15 the Bible says "Study to shew thyself approved unto God, a workman that needeth not to be ashamed, rightly dividing the word of truth. In order for us to develop into spiritual maturity we must continue to read and study God's word. We must know the Bible so we can apply it to our lives.

When new converts seek out a mentor they must know how to identify a worthy candidate. How can you identify a Seasoned Believer? Someone who will keep information confidential and someone who will not use the information to plot your demise.

A Seasoned Believer's Christian Walk will line up with their talk. They fear God and do not intentionally mistreat or harm people. They realize that if they mistreat or hurt people they are doing this to God because people are made in His image.

According to the Bible in Matthew 18:7, God warns those who intentionally hurt or put a stumbling block in another person's way. He says "Woe to the world because of its stumbling blocks! For it is inevitable that stumbling blocks come; but woe to that man through whom the stumbling block comes! (NAS)

In Matthew 7:22, Jesus rebuked those who thought they were doing God's Will. Jesus says in verse 22 to 23, "Many will say to Me on that day, Lord, Lord, did we not prophesy in your name, and in your name cast out demons, and in your name perform many miracles? And then I will declare to them, I never knew you; Depart from me, you who practice lawlessness. (NKJ)

When identifying Seasoned Believers you should use a spirit of discernment. You should also observe to see if a person's walk lines up with their talk. Seasoned Believers are those who are spiritually mature in the faith.

Although Seasoned Believers are students of the Bible, they are not perfect. They have flaws, forgiven sins, a previous history of inconsistencies and a desperate need like everyone else to serve the Lord. Seasoned Believers know that serving God is a daily challenge because we have an adversary, the devil, as a roaring lion, who walketh about, seeking whom he may devour. (1 Peter 5:8) The adversary is looking for those who are naive and weak in the Faith to plot their demise. He is a thief and his goal is to kill, steal and destroy. (John 10:10)

Seasoned Believers have a history of victories they can refer to when ministering to those who need encouragement. The devil has tried some of the same tactics with Seasoned Believers when they were babes in Christ. The Seasoned Believer is qualified to educate new converts on how to avoid some of the pitfalls that the enemy sets up.

The Seasoned Believer always strives to follow God's commandment in Titus 2:1-6. Older men are to train up the younger men and older women are to train up the younger women. A Seasoned Believer will possess six characteristics that will be covered in this book. Let's begin with Chapter I, Seasoned Believers Testify: You Must Be Born Again.

Seasoned Believers Testify
You Must Be Born Again

Chapter I

Seasoned Believers Testify You Must Be Born Again

Seasoned Believers are always ready to share the "Good News" about the Gospel with others. The "Good News" according to John 3:16 in the Bible is "For God so loved the world, that He gave his only begotten Son, that whosoever believeth in Him should not perish, but have everlasting life." In the book of John 3:17, it also goes on to say "For God sent not his Son into the world to condemn the world; but that the world through him might be saved."

All Christian Believers are responsible for spreading the "Good News" of the Gospel. It was the commission given to the disciples in Mark 16: 15-19. Jesus gave his disciples this commandment when he appeared to them after he had risen from the dead. He wanted to encourage the disciples because they did not believe those who had seen him after he rose from the dead.

When Jesus appeared to the disciples he said to them "Go ye into all the world, and preach the gospel to every creature. He that believeth and is baptized shall be saved; but he that believeth not shall be damned. And these signs shall follow them that believe; In my name shall they cast out devils; they shall speak with new tongues; They shall take up serpents; and if they drink any deadly thing, it shall not hurt them; they shall lay hands on the sick, and they shall recover." After Jesus gave his disciples the commission to go into the world and preach the gospel everywhere he was received up into heaven and sat on the right hand of God.

Seasoned Believers understand that it is important for everyone to hear about the "Good News" of the Gospel. Everyone must know about Jesus because he was sacrificed for the sins of the world. According to Wikipedia.com, the gospel was the good news of redemption through the propitiatory offering of Jesus Christ for one's sins, the central Christian message which is found in John 3:16.

Seasoned Believers also testify that you must be born again. To understand what it means to be born-again, it is necessary to understand that there are TWO BIRTHS. The "first" birth is the PHYSICAL BIRTH when you were born into this world from your mother and father. When the Bible speaks of being "born of water," it is speaking about the physical birth NOT baptism. The "second" birth is a SPIRITUAL BIRTH, which means to be born of the "Spirit" that is, God's Holy Spirit. (Paster Harry A. Ironside)

An example of the two births are given in the Bible in John 3:1-7. "There was a man of the Pharisees, name Nicodemus, a ruler of the Jews; The same came to Jesus by night, and said unto him, Rabbi, we know that thou art a teacher come from God: for no man can do these miracles that thou doest, except God be with him. Jesus answered and said unto him, Verily, verily, I say unto thee, Except a man be born again, he cannot see the kingdom of God. Nicodemus saith unto him, How can a man be born when he is old? Can he enter the second time into his mother's womb, and he be born? Jesus answered, Verily, verily, I say unto thee, Except a man be born of water and of the Spirit, he cannot enter the kingdom of God. That which is born of the flesh is flesh; and that which is born of the Spirit is spirit. Marvel not that I said unto thee, Ye must be born again. The wind bloweth where it listeth, and thou hearest the sound thereof, but canst not tell whence it cometh, and whither it goeth; so is every one that is born of the spirit.

Seasoned Believers testify that you must be baptized with the Holy Ghost and receive power. According to Acts 1:1-5, 7-8, Jesus promised his disciples that they would be baptized with the Holy Ghost. He assured them that when they were baptized by the Holy Ghost they would receive power and become his witnesses in Jerusalem, Judea, Samaria and to the remotest part of the earth. In Acts 2:1-4 Jesus promise to the disciples was fulfilled on the Day of Pentecost.

Seasoned Believers also testify about the power of the Holy Ghost and what the power enables us to do. According to Acts 2:17-21 it says "And it shall come to pass in the last days, saith God, I will pour out my Spirit upon all flesh: and your sons and your daughters shall prophesy, and your young men shall see visions, and your old men shall dream dreams: And on my servants and on my handmaidens I will pour out in those days of my Spirit; and they shall prophesy: And I will shew wonders in heaven above, and signs in the earth beneath; blood, and fire, and vapour of smoke: The sun shall be turned into darkness, and the moon into blood, before the great and notable day of the Lord come: And it shall come to pass, that whosoever shall call on the name of the Lord shall be saved.

Seasoned Believers are *Eye Witnesses* about the goodness of God. They have creditable information or personal testimonies about how God delivered, healed or blessed them. Seasoned Believers can testify about their own trials and tribulations of how they came through and overcame them all. Believers will go through trials and tribulations in life. They will also be tested and tried by the enemy which is Satan. Believers overcome the enemy in their trials and tribulations by the blood of the lamb and by the words of their testimonies. (Revelation 12:11)

When reporters write a news story they look for eye

witnesses. Those who were on the scene when the event took place. Reporters look for those who know the facts and can add creditable information to their story. They want their story to be factual and have integrity. Seasoned Believers stand behind what they say, what they do and are bold in their testimony.

Seasoned Believers can testify that there is no other way but to be born again. Unless a person is born of the spirit he or she is still carnal minded and cannot perceive the things of the spirit. The carnal mind is not spiritually minded because it is at war against God. (Romans 8:7) You make yourself an enemy of God when you become friends with the world. (James 4:4) God is a jealous God. (Exodus 34:14) You cannot serve two Gods or two masters according to Joshua 24:15 and Matthew 6:24.

It is a testimony against believers when others cannot see the difference between a believer's behavior and the behavior of those in the world. Many call this backsliding. Backsliding is when a believer allows their lust or sin to carry them away from God. When believers return to a lifestyle of sin the bible says in Hebrews 6:4-6 "For it is impossible for those who were once enlightened, and have tasted of the heavenly gift, and were made partakers of the Holy Ghost. And have tasted the good word of God, and the powers of the world to come, If they shall fall away, to renew them again unto repentance; seeing they crucify to themselves the Son of God afresh, and put him to an open shame. Pure religion and undefiled before God and the Father is this, To visit the fatherless and widows in their affliction, and to keep himself unspotted from the world. (James 1:27)

Testimony:

As a child growing up, I learned a lot from Seasoned Believers who God brought into my life. I was baptized at a young age. My mom took my sister, brother and I to Sunday School and Church regularly in her hometown. When we moved to Dallas, Texas we no longer attended church.

When I was in high school, I remember having a hunger to read God's word like never before. I took my Bible and read it on the bus. I also remember one Sunday I woke up, got dressed and went to the first church I saw. I joined and rededicated my life to the Lord.

I remember a woman named Laura who I met in church. She was a student of the Bible. She seemed to take an interest in me as a teenager. She gave me her own personal Bible so I could read the scriptures. She became my mentor. There was one question I had for her. I remember as a child growing up I would hear other believers talking about being baptized by the fire. They would also say you need to be baptized by the Spirit.

I wanted to know what that meant. When our church went to a revival one Sunday, I asked Ms. Laura what does it mean to be baptized by the fire or baptized by the spirit? She asked, "Do you want to find out?" I said, "yes."

She took me to the altar when the evangelist called people down for prayer. As we stood at the altar Ms. Laura told me to lift my hands and bow my head. She began to pray for me. While she was praying tears were streaming from my eyes as I was crying out to God. I didn't know what it all meant at the time it was happening. When we left the altar that day, I still had questions about that experience and what happened to me. I knew something happened to me that I never experienced before.

As I continued to pray and study God's word, I developed a deeper relationship with God. Later as a young adult I found out through studying the scriptures and other mentors that I was baptized by the Spirit. I was born again and filled with the Holy Spirit.

Further Study:

For the wages of sin is death; but the gift of God is eternal life through Jesus Christ our Lord. (Romans 6:23)

If we confess our sins, he is faithful and just to forgive us our sins, and to cleanse us from all unrighteousness. (1 John 1:9)

Bless the Lord, O my soul, and forget not all his benefits: Who forgiveth all thine iniquities; who healeth all thy diseases; Who redeemeth thy life from destruction; who crowneth thee with lovingkindness and tender mercies. (Psalms 103:2-4)

Christ hath redeemed us from the curse of the law, being made a curse for us: for it is written, Cursed is every one that hangeth on a tree. (Galatians 3:13)

Seasoned Believers Point You To The Word Of God For Truth

Chapter II

Seasoned Believers Point You To The Word Of God For Truth

Seasoned Believers point us to the word of God and give us the unadulterated truth. They serve as mentors and give advice based on the Bible. Seasoned Believers will always point you back to the word of God so you can know the Bible for yourself. Knowing the Bible will help prevent you from being mislead or brainwashed by someone else. Ye shall know the truth and the truth shall make you free according to John 8:32.

John 17:17 says "Thy word is truth." Many young believers or babes in Christ rely on someone to lead them into all truth. They reverence another man's word instead of the word of God. It is important to study to shew thyself approved unto God, a workman that needeth not to be ashamed, rightly dividing the word of truth. (2 Timothy 2:15)

In Acts 17:11 the people of Berea were excited about receiving the word of God from Paul and Silas. They received the word with readiness of mind and they searched the scriptures daily to see if the things they were told were true.

The Bereans are an example to young believers or babes in Christ. They should be ready to receive the word of God and also search the Bible for themselves. Seasoned Believers testify to young believers or babes in Christ that the Holy Ghost will lead them into all truth. The Holy Ghost is the promised helper that Jesus told his disciples about. "Howbeit when he, the Spirit of truth, is come, he will guide you into all truth: for he shall not speak of himself; but whatsoever he shall hear, that shall he speak: and he will shew you things to come. (John 16:13) The Holy Ghost is very active in believers today.

Seasoned Believers instruct us and point us to the word of God in how we should live after we are born again and have received the Holy Ghost. The Holy Ghost is our helper and teaches us how to live life. In Galatians 5:16-18 it reads "This I say then, Walk in the Spirit and ye shall not fulfill the lust of the flesh. For the flesh lusteth against the Spirit, and the Spirit against the flesh: and these are contrary the one to the other: so that ye cannot do the things that ye would. But if ye be led of the Spirit, ye are not under the law."

When we walk in the Spirit, we will not fulfill the desires of the flesh. According to Galatians 5:19-21 the deeds of the flesh are immorality, impurity, sensuality, idolatry, sorcery, enmities, strife, jealousy, outbursts of anger, disputes, dissensions, factions, envying, drunkenness, carousing. The Bible says that those who practice the deeds previously mentioned will not inherit the kingdom of God.

When we walk in the Spirit, we exhibit the fruits of the Spirit which are love, joy, peace, patience, kindness, goodness, faithfulness, gentleness, self-control; against such there is no law according to Galatians 5:22-23. In Galatians 5:25-26 we are further admonished to live and walk in the Spirit. We should not desire vain glory, provoke or envy one another.

God's word helps us to be successful as we walk out the plan He has for our lives. His word is powerful and living. According to Hebrews 4:12 "For the word of God is quick, and powerful, and sharper than any two edged sword, piercing even to the dividing asunder of soul and spirit, and of the joints and marrow, and is a discerner of the thoughts and intents of the heart."

God's word is your guide and road map. It will help you in dark and uncertain places of your life. Psalm 119:105 says "Thy word is a lamp unto my feet, and a light unto my path." God's word has His promises and assures the believer that He is concerned about His children. God loved us when He sent His son to die on the cross as a sacrifice for sins of the world. We should love God by hiding His word in our hearts, so we won't sin against Him. (Psalm 119:11)

Seasoned Believers or mentors want the best for who they mentor. Their relationship with the one they mentor is not based on them getting something from the mentee. They realize they are the teacher and the giver who will pour into the one who needs mentoring.

Seasoned Believers give advice to help keep you out of trouble. They have life experiences their mentee can benefit from. The Bible says in Proverbs 11:14, "Where no counsel is, the people fall: but in the multitude of counselors there is safety." The older men are to teach the younger men and the older women are to teach the younger women according to Titus 2:1-6.

Season Believers have practical instruction. They don't lead babes in Christ to think the Christian Journey will be easy or magical. For precept must be upon precept, precept upon precept; line upon line, line upon line; here a little, and there a little. (Isaiah 28:10) Seasoned Believers explain how things are done and there is no deception in it. The Seasoned Believer's life is a testimony of his or her success. Seasoned Believers are willing to share how God helped and blessed them in their efforts. Babes in Christ will learn that God has a plan for each of us and everyone has their season to excel. (Ecclesiastes 3)

Seasoned Believers may not be popular with the crowd, but you can count on them to tell you right from wrong.

Seasoned Believers don't wear masks. They are consistent in who they are and what they do and say. Seasoned Believers are constant and anchored in the word of God. You can count on them to be who they testify they are. They are mature and seasoned and are not tossed to and fro by every wind and doctrine. They check things against scriptures and research things out before they jump behind the newest trend. They will tell you the truth about your situation if asked for their advice. They will not lie to you to be your friend. Seasoned Believers will challenge you to spiritually grow.

Seasoned Believers are responsible and judge themselves before God has to judge them. When Seasoned Believers do fall, they repent and get back on track with God. Seasoned Believers don't blame their actions and behavior on someone else. They take responsibility for their lives.

Testimony:

Living the Christian Life will not always be easy, especially when you encounter tests and trials. During these times we should always pray without ceasing. (1 Thessalonians 5:17) We should rely on the Holy Spirit to lead us in our decisions. The Holy Spirit will lead us into all truth. (John 16:13) We need to also depend on the Bible to help guide us. Thy word is truth. (John 17:17)

During times when I encounter tests and trials the Holy Spirit brings to my remembrance those scriptures that apply to my situation. God also uses people to bring clarification to help answer my questions. God uses Believers who point me back to His word. I have learned in whatever trial or test I encounter I can depend on God to lead me in the right direction.

Further Study:

Thy word is truth (John 17:17)

So shall my word be that goeth forth out of my mouth: it shall not return unto me void, but it shall accomplish that which I please, and it shall prosper in the thing whereto I sent it. (Isaiah 55:11)

Then said the Lord unto me, Thou hast well seen: for I will hasten my word to perform it. (Jeremiah 1:12)

Fear not, little flock; for it is your Father's good pleasure to give you the kingdom. (Luke 12:32)

Let them shout for joy, and be glad, that favour my righteous cause: yea, let them say continually, Let the Lord be magnified, which hath pleasure in the prosperity of his servant. (Psalm 35:27)

And Joseph said unto them, Fear not: for am I in the place of God? But as for you, ye thought evil against me; but God meant it unto good, to bring to pass, as it is this day, to save much people alive. (Genesis 50:19-20)

And we know that all things work together for good to them that love God, to them who are the called according to his purpose. (Romans 8:28)

It is he that sitteth upon the circle of the earth, and the inhabitants thereof are as grasshoppers; that stretcheth out the heavens as a curtain, and spreadeth them out as a tent to dwell in: That bringeth the princes to nothing; he maketh the judges of the earth as vanity. (Isaiah 40:22-23)

I waited patiently for the Lord; and he inclined unto me, and heard my cry. He brought me up also out of an horrible pit, out of the miry clay, and set my feet upon a rock, and established my goings. And he hath put a new song in my mouth, even praise unto our God: many shall see it, and fear, and shall trust in the Lord. (Psalm 40:1-3)

And they overcame him by the blood of the Lamb, and by the word of their testimony; and they loved not their lives unto the death. (Revelation 12:11)

No weapon that is formed against thee shall prosper; and every tongue that shall rise against thee in judgment thou shalt condemn. This is the heritage of the servants of the Lord, and their righteousness is of me, saith the Lord. (Isaiah 54:17)

If any of you lack wisdom, let him ask of God, that giveth to all men liberally, and upbraideth not; and it shall be given him. (James 1:5)

Seasoned Believers Come And Bear

.

Chapter III

Seasoned Believers Come And Bear

The third quality of a Seasoned Believer is their compassion to come and bear the burdens of others. Romans 15:1-3 says "Now we that are strong ought to bear the infirmities of the weak, and not to please ourselves. Let each one of us please his neighbor for that which is good, unto edifying. For Christ who pleased not himself, but as it is written, the reproaches of them that reproached thee fell upon me." According to dictionary.com, to bear means to hold up or support. Seasoned Believers support you in practical ways during your time of need and are able to give you God's word for wisdom. They are not fair-weather friends. Fair weather friends are those who come around when the weather is non- threatening or when times are good. They disappear when thunderstorms come in your life. They leave when times are bad and when you need them most. When Seasoned Believers see someone in need or can lighten someone's load, they do it without grumbling and with a kind heart.

Seasoned Believers do not take advantage of someone they were sent to help. While helping those who are weak, Season Believers do not have hidden agendas or rob people out of their resources. When someone is weak and vulnerable, they need someone to trust until they regain strength. Seasoned Believers are not opportunists who swindle people who are too weak to defend or think for themselves. A swindler according to Dictionary.com is anyone who cheats a person or business out of money or assets. They use plausible schemes or unscrupulous trickery to defraud others. Plausible is having an appearance of truth or reason seemingly worthy of approval or acceptance. It is creditable and believable.

An example of the behavior of a swindler can be found in Genesis 25:29-34. "And Jacob sod pottage: and Esau came from the field, and he *was* faint: And Esau said to Jacob, Feed me, I pray thee, with that same red *pottage*; for I *am* faint: therefore was his name called Edom. And Jacob said, Sell me this day thy birthright. And Esau said, Behold, I *am* at the point to die: and what profit shall this birthright do to me? And Jacob said, Swear to me this day; and he sware unto him: and he sold his birthright unto Jacob. Then Jacob gave Esau bread and pottage of lentiles; and he did eat and drink, and rose up, and went his way: thus Esau despised *his* birthright."

Even though Esau did not care much about his birthright he was still the first-born son. With this position comes many blessings that Esau did not regret until later.

Esau was hungry and was helped by his brother Jacob at a dear price. Jacob took advantage of his brother's temporary state of hunger and swindled him out of his birth right. Later Esau regretted he made a permanent decision based on a temporary situation.

Hebrews 12:16-17 states "lest there *be* any fornicator or profane person like Esau, who for one morsel of food sold his birthright. For you know that afterward, when he wanted to inherit the blessing, he was rejected, for he found no place for repentance, though he sought it diligently with tears." Seasoned Believers are trustworthy when it comes to handling someone else's business or resources.

Seasoned Believers do not seize an opportunity to prey on the weak. They are not swindlers who manipulate those who are under their care for ministry. It is not good to use your position of trust to hurt, manipulate or mislead someone when you know they trust you. When those who are weak regain strength they will never trust those who took advantage of them again.

Some have perfected the craft of swindling people out of their resources. They have lead people astray by intentionally giving wrong information. The wrong information ultimately hurts their victims. Swindlers are among the ones who will not inherit the kingdom of God according to 1 Corinthians 6:9-10.

Seasoned Believers know their role when they come to bear another's burdens. Seasoned Believers don't look for compensation when helping those who are unable to help themselves. They allow God to reward them when it is necessary without manipulation. This is very important because you want to allow people to be strong enough to make their own decisions when it comes to giving of their resources.

Testimony:

As a young bride I became a widow at 23 years old. I remember taking care of my husband who was terminally ill. During that time, I continued to work, go to college and care for my husband. When he finally passed away, I was so tired and drained. God used me to bear the infirmities of my husband during his weakness. In the same fashion, God sent people who knew of my situation to bear my infirmities during my time of weakness. People came to nurture and encourage me until I was strong again. Seasoned Believers come to bear the infirmities of the weak.

Further Study:

For God hath not given us the spirit of fear, but of power, and of love, and of a sound mind. (2 Timothy 1:7)

For with God nothing shall be impossible. (Luke 1:37)

Surely, he shall deliver thee from the snare of the fowler, and from the noisome pestilence. (Psalms 91:3)

Though I walk in the midst of trouble, thou wilt revive me: thou shalt stretch forth thine hand against the wrath of mine enemies, and thy right hand shall save me. The Lord will perfect that which concerneth me: thy mercy, O Lord, endureth for ever: forsake not the works of thine own hands. (Psalms 138:7-8)

Notwithstanding the Lord stood with me, and strengthened me; that by me the preaching might be fully known, and that all the Gentiles might hear: and I was delivered out of the mouth of the lion. And the Lord shall deliver me from every evil work, and will preserve me unto his heavenly kingdom:

to whom be glory forever and ever. Amen. (2 Timothy 4:17-18)

The Lord is my rock, and my fortress, and my deliverer; my God, my strength, in whom I will trust; my buckler, and the horn of my salvation, and my high tower. I will call upon the Lord, who is worthy to be praised: so shall I be saved from mine enemies. (Psalms 18:2-3)

I Shall not die, but live, and declare the works of the Lord. (Psalm 118:17)

No weapon that is formed against thee shall prosper; and every tongue that shall rise against thee in judgment thou shalt condemn. This is the heritage of the servants of the Lord, and their righteousness is of me, saith the Lord. (Isaiah 54:17)

If ye abide in me, and my words abide in you, ye shall ask what ye will, and it shall be done unto you. (John 15:7)

Verily, verily, I say unto you, He that believeth on me, the works that I do shall he do also; and greater works than these shall he do; because I go unto my Father. And whatsoever ye shall ask in my name, that will I do, that the Father may be glorified in the Son. If ye shall ask any thing in my name, I will do it. (John 14:12-14)

God is not a man, that he should lie, neither the son of man, that he should repent: hath he said, and shall he not do it? Or hath he spoken, and shall he not make it good? (Numbers 23:19)

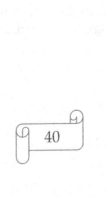

Seasoned Believers Remind You and Encourage

Chapter IV

Seasoned Believers Remind You and Encourage

The fifth quality of a Seasoned Believer is to remind and encourage others. Seasoned Believers enjoy encouraging others and they remind you of God's promises.

The Christian walk is full of joy, but it will not always be easy. There are times of disappointments and setbacks as you pursue a victorious Christian life. You will have to make right choices to get the blessings God has pre-ordained for you.

There will be times of disappointments, but this is not the time to give up and throw in the towel. New Believers sometimes start their new life as a Christian with much eager and joy. They are excited about the new life they have chosen to follow Jesus Christ. The enemy is not a fan of your new life in Christ. He will put stumbling blocks in your way to make you abandon living the victorious Christian life. It is inevitable that stumbling blocks will come according to Luke 17:1. There are some new Believers who start off living a victorious Christian Life then they get discouraged at the first sign of trouble. Christ is always concerned about you and wants you to be victorious.

As a New Believer you should have a valid reason why you have decided to follow Jesus Christ. It is defined as your testimony or the reason that brought you to Christ. 1 Peter 3:15 says "But sanctify the Lord God in your hearts: and be ready always to give an answer to every man that asketh you a reason of the hope that is in you with meakness and fear."

Season Believers encourage new converts who are ridiculed, given misinformation and who are discouraged in their Christian faith. Like the Apostle Paul, Seasoned Believers remind new converts of the reason why they decided to serve Jesus Christ. In Galatians 5:7-10 it states "You were running a good race, who cut in on you and kept you from obeying the truth? That kind of persuasion does not come from the one who calls you. A little yeast worketh through the whole batch of dough. I am confident in the Lord that you will take no other view. The one who is throwing you into confusion will pay the penalty, whoever he may be."

Seasoned Believers also help new converts stand firm in their faith. They remind them "It is for freedom that Christ has set us free. Stand firm, then, and do not let yourselves be burdened again by a yoke of slavery." (Galatians 5:1)

Seasoned Believers also remind new converts not to be careless with their freedom they have in Christ. Just like Paul reminded the Galatians he said "You, my brothers, were called to be free. But do not use your freedom to indulge the sinful nature, rather, serve one another in love." (Galatians 5:13)

The Seasoned Believer also reminds new converts that God does not do things like man according to Isaiah 55:8. It says, "For my thoughts *are* not your thoughts, neither *are* your ways my ways, saith the LORD."

Seasoned Believers remind new converts that it is better to listen and take head the first time around. Enter ye in at the strait gate: for wide *is* the gate, and broad *is* the way, that leadeth to destruction, and many there be which go in thereat: Because strait *is* the gate, and narrow *is* the way, which leadeth unto life, and few there be that find it. (Matthew 7:13-14)

Seasoned Believers educate new converts by explaining spiritual and natural laws God put into place before the beginning of time. These laws still exist and operate the way God intended. Spiritual and Natural Laws will continue to do what God had ordained them to do. No man can change God's order of things or manipulate the spiritual and natural laws of the universe. Even when man does try to manipulate the spiritual and natural laws God's word still holds true.

According to Psalm 37:1-2, it says "Fret not thyself because of evildoers, neither be thou envious against the workers of iniquity. For they shall soon be cut down like the grass, and wither as the green herb." God is serious when it comes to reaping and sowing and obeying and respecting Spiritual and Natural Laws.

Seasoned Believers also remind new converts that it is important to pay attention to their Christian walk and do self evaluations. For if we would judge ourselves, we should not be judged. But when we are judged, we are chastened of the Lord, that we should not be condemned with the world. (1 Cor. 11:31-32)

Testimony:

There are times when disappointments weigh me down. Contemplating on where I went wrong and how to correct things occupies me until I hear from God. God always sends someone who understands my dilemma. That person is also able to give God's word for encouragement. There are times when God brings a scripture to my remembrance that sheds lights on my situation. I can truly say God never fails me during my time of despair.

Further Study:

Trust in the Lord with all thine heart; and lean not unto thine own understanding. In all thy ways acknowledge him, and he shall direct thy paths. (Proverbs 3:5-6)

Be careful for nothing; but in everything by prayer and supplication with thanksgiving let your requests be made known unto God. And the peace of God, which passeth all understanding, shall keep your hearts and minds through Christ Jesus. (Philippians 4:6-7)

The steps of a good man are ordered by the Lord: and he delighteth in his way. (Psalms 37:23)

Seek ye the Lord while he may be found, call ye upon him while he is near: (Isaiah 55:6)

There is a way that seemeth right unto a man, but the end thereof are the ways of death. (Proverbs 16:25)

Be still, and know that I am God: I will be exalted among the heathen, I will be exalted in the earth. (Psalms 46:10)

Thy word is a lamp unto my feet, and a light unto my path. (Psalms 119:105)

And thine ears shall hear a word behind thee, saying, This is the way, walk ye in it, when ye turn to the right hand, and when ye turn to the left. (Isaiah 30:21)

I will instruct thee and teach thee in the way which thou shalt go: I will guide thee with mine eye. (Psalm 32:8)

The righteousness of the perfect shall direct his way: but the wicked shall fall by his own wickedness. (Proverbs 11:5) For his God doth instruct him to discretion, and doth teach him. (Isaiah 28:26)

A man's heart deviseth his way: but the Lord directeth his steps. (Proverbs 16:9)

For this God is our God forever and ever: he will be our guide even unto death. (Psalms 48:14)

I must work the works of him that sent me, while it is day: the night cometh, when no man can work. (John 9:4)

Seasoned Believers Expose Sin And Enlighten About Its Effects

Chapter V

Seasoned Believers Expose Sin And Enlighten About Its Effects

The fifth quality of a Seasoned Believer is to expose sin and enlighten about the effects of it. Seasoned Believers are bold when confronting sin and speaking what is right. They do not bite their tongue when it comes to speaking what God tells them to.

When new converts begin living a victorious Christian life, sometimes they are unaware of the struggles of their sin nature. Some Christians have become sick as a result of sin. According to James 5:14-16 it says "Is any among you sick? Let him call for the elders of the church; and let them pray over him, anointing him with oil in the name of the Lord: and the prayer of faith shall save him that is sick, and the Lord shall raise him up: and if he have committed sins, it shall be forgiven him. Confess therefore your sins one to another, and pray one for another, that ye may be healed. The supplication of a righteous man availeth much in its working."

Seasoned Believers exhort us to repent of sin and get back on track with God. In I John 1:9-10 it says "If we confess our sins, he is faithful and righteous to forgive us our sins, and to cleanse us from all unrighteousness. If we say that we have not sinned, we make him a liar, and his word is not in us."

Sometimes when new converts fall into sin, they feel their iniquities are beyond forgiveness. Seasoned Believers continue to encourage and remind new Believers of the word of God. In 1 John 2:1-2 it says "My little children, these things I write unto you that ye may not sin. And if any man sin, we have an Advocate with the Father, Jesus Christ the righteous: and he is the propitiation for our sins, and not for ours only, but also for the whole world."

Seasoned Believers know that new converts will go astray. They must be lead back to the path of the straight and narrow. James 5:19-20 says "My brethren, if any among you err from the truth, and one convert him; let him know, that he who converteth a sinner from the error of his way shall save a soul from death, and shall cover a multitude of sins."

Seasoned Believers help new believers figure out why they get certain repetitive results in their lives. The principle of sowing and reaping is explained in Galatians 6:7-9 which reads "Do not be deceived. God cannot be mocked. A man reaps what he sows. The one who sows to please his sinful nature, from that nature will reap destruction; the one who sows to please the Spirit, from the Spirit will reap eternal life. Let us not become weary in doing good, for at the proper time we will reap a harvest if we do not give up."

Seasoned Believers also help new Believers when they explain the penalty of continuing in sin after they have been warned. Hebrews 10:26-31 explains what will happen if their sinful behavior continues. "For if we sin willfully after that we have received the knowledge of the truth, there remaineth no more a sacrifice for sins, but a certain fearful expectation of judgement, and a fierceness of fire which shall devour the adversaries. A man that hath set at nought Moses law dieth without compassion on the word of two or three witnesses; of how much sorer punishment, think ye, shall he be judged worthy, who hath trodden under foot the Son of God, and hath counted the blood of the covenant wherewith he was sanctified an unholy thing, and hath done despite unto the Spirit of grace?"

Seasoned Believers also assures the new converts that according to Hebrews 10: 30-31 that it is God who will judge. "For we know him and said, Vengeance belongeth unto me, I will recompense, And again, The Lord shall judge his people. It is a fearful thing to fall into the hands of the living God."

Seasoned Believers remind new converts they cannot run the Christian race victoriously unless they let go of things that keep them in sin. According to Hebrews 12:1-2, it says "Wherefore seeing we also are compassed about with so great a cloud of witnesses, let us lay aside every weight, and the sin which doth so easily beset *us*, and let us run with patience the race that is set before us, Looking unto Jesus the author and finisher of *our* faith; who for the joy that was set before him endured the cross, despising the shame, and is set down at the right hand of the throne of God."

Our journey will be rough if we continue to hold on to things that weigh us down and keep us in sin. We will not have success if we continue to rebel against God's word. Good understanding giveth favour: but the way of transgressors *is* hard. (Proverbs 13:15)

Testimony:

Therefore, to him that knoweth to do good, and doeth it not, to him it is sin. (James 4:17) When we do not follow God's word concerning marriage we will suffer heartache. God wants us to be equally yoked when it comes to marriage. When a believer marries an unbeliever it can cause misery for everyone involved especially children. When the marriage ends in divorce it causes more pain and suffering on the family. It is important to follow God's plan for marriage.

Further Study:

For whom the Lord loveth he correcteth; even as a father the son in whom he delighteth. (Proverbs 3:12)

Behold, happy is the man whom God correcteth: therefore despise not thou the chastening of the Almighty: For he maketh sore, and bindeth up: he woundeth, and his hands make whole. (Job 5:17-18)

Blessed is the man whom thou chastenest, O Lord, and teachest him out of thy law; that thou mayest give him rest from the days of adversity, until the pit be digged for the wicked. (Psalms 94:12-13)

But when we are judged, we are chastened of the Lord, that we should not be condemned with the world. (1 Corinthians 11:32)

For whom the Lord loveth he chasteneth, and scourgeth every son whom he receiveth. If ye endure chastening, God dealeth with you as with sons; for what son is he whom the father chasteneth not? (Hebrews 12:6-7)

For they verily for a few days chastened us after their own pleasure; but he for our profit, that we might be partakers of his holiness. Now no chastening for the present seemeth to be joyous, but grievous: nevertheless afterward it yieldeth the peaceable fruit of righteousness unto them which are exercised thereby. (Hebrews 12:10-11)

For the wages of sin is death; but the gift of God is eternal life through Jesus Christ our Lord. (Romans 6:23)

Who gave himself for our sins, that he might deliver us from this present evil world, according to the will of God and our Father. (Galatians 1:4)

For the Lord God is a sun and shield: the Lord will give grace and glory: no good thing will he withhold from them that walk uprightly. (Psalms 84:11)

For he that eateth and drinketh unworthily, eateth and drinketh damnation to himself, not discerning the Lord's body. For this cause many are weak and sickly among you, and many sleep. For if we would judge ourselves, we should not be judged. But when we are judged, we are chastened of the Lord, that we should not be condemned with the world. (1 Corinthians 11:29-32)

But God is the judge: he putteth down one, and setteth up another. (Psalms 75:7)

For if we sin wilfully after that we have received the knowledge of the truth, there remaineth no more sacrifice for sins, But a certain fearful looking for of judgment and fiery indignation, which shall devour the adversaries. (Hebrews 10:26-27)

And even as they did not like to retain God in their knowledge, God gave them over to a reprobate mind, to do those things which are not convenient. (Romans 1:28)

The Lord shall send upon thee cursing, vexation, and rebuke, in all that thou settest thine hand unto for to do, until thou be destroyed, and until thou perish quickly; because of the wickedness of thy doings, whereby thou hast forsaken me. (Deuteronomy 28:20)

Be not deceived; God is not mocked: for whatsoever a man soweth, that shall he also reap. (Galatians 6:7)

Seasoned Believers Come And Restore

Chapter VI

Seasoned Believers Come And Restore

The sixth quality of a Seasoned Believer is to restore others who have sinned and fallen away from the faith. They come to restore and rebuild. They don't come to destroy and do further damage to the fallen Believer. Seasoned Believers are ambassadors for Christ. Remember Jesus says, "the thief cometh not, but for to steal, and to kill, and to destroy, I am come that they might have life, and that they might have *it* more abundantly" (John 10:10)

Seasoned Believers do not come to inflict pain or cause you to experience a hopeless situation in the name of God. According to James 1:17 "Every good gift and every perfect gift is from above, and cometh down from the Father of lights, with whom is no variableness, neither shadow of turning." It also states in Proverbs 10:22 "The blessing of the LORD, it maketh rich, and he addeth no sorrow with it." If you receive something that causes you to have much sorrow it is not a blessing from God.

Seasoned Believers restore fallen believers and remind them of God's love. They also explain the importance of repentance to receive forgiveness. The Seasoned Believer is concerned about getting the fallen believer back into the fold. It is the responsibility of the spiritually mature to restore those who have fallen according to Galatians 6:1. It reads "Brethren, if a man be overtaken in a fault, ye which are spiritual, restore such a one in the spirit of meekness; considering thyself, lest thou also be tempted.

Seasoned Believers are wise and know that anyone can be tempted and overtaken in a fault. Seasoned Believers know that the Christian Journey is a battle and one must follow the straight and narrow road. Matthew 7:13 admonishes us to "Enter ye in at the strait gate: for wide *is* the gate, and broad *is* the way, that leadeth to destruction, and many there be which go in thereat:"

Seasoned Believers know from experience that new Believers will fall into destruction because of wrong choices. They will sometimes become prey to the enemy when they are babes in Christ, weak, and naive. The enemy loves to bring stumbling blocks to hinder new converts. As Believers we can rest assure that God will deal with our enemies and the stumbling blocks that are set in place to make us fall. Jesus addressed this very concern with his disciples. "He said, "It is inevitable that stumbling blocks come, but woe to him through whom they come!" (Luke 17:1 ASV)

Seasoned Believers know new converts will encounter enemies who stir up wrath. The new convert has to learn not to retaliate in anger. It is sometimes hard to hold back wrath when the enemy is working through someone to cause malice and strife. As Believers we must keep our focus on God. We should always pray and not faint. We must meditate on His word day and night. We must also hide His word in our hearts that we might not sin against HIM. God's way is always right. For the wrath of man worketh not the righteousness of God. (James 1:20)

Seasoned Believers restore fallen believers so they can be strong again and return to their first love. Seasoned Believers help fallen believers renew their zeal for the father. Seasoned Believers know the enemy works through anyone whether it is family, friends or foes. There are some who have decided not to trust God. They become irritated by people who trust God. Those who rebel against God become jealous when they see the favor of God on other people. The rebellious have the wrong view and understanding of God. Things would change if they accept Jesus Christ in their heart as Lord and Savior. They can develop a personal relationship with God for themselves and experience the same joy.

Paul encouraged the Galatians when they were troubled. Paul said in Galatians 5:7-10 "You were running a good race, who cut in on you and kept you from obeying the truth? That kind of persuasion does not come from the one who calls you. A little yeast worketh through the whole batch of dough. I am confident in the Lord that you will take no other view. The one who is throwing you into confusion will pay the penalty, whoever he may be."

Seasoned Believers continue to mentor new converts about the schemes of the devil. The enemy is very crafty and wants to destroy those who name the name of Jesus Christ. The enemy wants to discredit, humiliate, harm, and destroy. The enemy does not care which vessel he uses. He just wants to overthrow God's purpose for your life. It is up to the Believer to trust God and walk in the Spirit and not in the flesh. The flesh will react to the motives, the harsh words and the behavior of those who want Believers to fail. Seasoned Believers model the example of Christ. They are shrewd as serpents and innocent as doves. (Matthew 10:16 NAS)

Seasoned Believers are firm when it comes to dealing with the enemy. They are spiritually mature and have been tried and tested. They are victorious on many levels. They continue to study God's word and keep a close and intimate relationship with God. Seasoned Believers are wise in this according to 2 Corinthians 2:11 "so that no advantage would be taken of us by Satan, for we are not ignorant of his schemes." Seasoned Believers also carry themselves as mature adults in the faith. They can declare "That we *henceforth* be no more children, tossed to and fro, and carried about with every wind of doctrine, by the sleight of men, *and* cunning craftiness, whereby they lie in wait to deceive;" (Ephesians 4:14)

New Believers must be committed to developing their own personal relationship with God to grow into spiritual maturity. They must be lead by the spirit and not the flesh. They must study God's word and obey it. New Believers must follow after and seek truth. They should fellowship with other believers, be accountable and repent when they sin, learn from their mistakes and grow in God's grace.

Testimony:

I experienced a lot of sorrow when I trusted two mechanics to fix my car. I paid money to have it fixed but was disappointed with the results. The lack of accountability of both mechanics left my family walking. Even though I pleaded with both mechanics it fell on deaf ears. God turned things around when I was referred to a certified repair shop with certified mechanics who guaranteed their labor.

The lesson I learned is to always take my car to a certified shop with certified mechanics. Get estimates and guarantees in writing for parts and labor. Always ask to retrieve your old parts when having a part replaced on your car. Ask for a receipt with itemized costs for parts and labor. Always take your car back to the shop if you are still having problems. If there is no resolution, then the mechanic shop and mechanics must be held accountable by taking legal action.

Further Study:

But I say unto you, Love your enemies, bless them that curse you, do good to them that hate you, and pray for them which despitefully use you, and persecute you; That ye may be the children of your Father which is in heaven: for he maketh his sun to rise on the evil and on the good, and sendeth rain on the just and on the unjust. (Matthew 5:44-45)

And when ye stand praying, forgive, if ye have ought against any: that your Father also which is in heaven may forgive you your trespasses. But if ye do not forgive, neither will your Father which is in heaven forgive your trespasses. (Mark 11:25-26)

Therefore if thine enemy hunger, feed him; if he thirst, give him drink: for in so doing thou shalt heap coals of fire on his head. (Romans 12:20)

Say not thou, I will recompense evil; but wait on the Lord, and he shall save thee. (Proverbs 20:22)

If we confess our sins, he is faithful and just to forgive us our sins, and to cleanse us from all unrighteousness. (1 John 1:9)

Bless the Lord, O my soul, and forget not all his benefits: Who forgiveth all thine iniquities; who healeth all thy diseases; Who redeemeth thy life from destruction; who crowneth thee with lovingkindness and tender mercies. (Psalms 103:2-4)

Christ hath redeemed us from the curse of the law, being made a curse for us: for it is written, Cursed is every one that hangeth on a tree. (Galatians 3:13)

Conclusion

Conclusion

Conclusion

Pass The Salt Please! Seasoned Believers Add Flavor To Your Life is a guide to help new converts grow into Christian maturity. New converts are ultimately responsible for their own spiritual growth. Studying the Bible, developing a personal relationship with God, fellowshipping with other believers, being lead by the Holy Spirit, obedience to God's word, repentance, and growing in grace are all included in your experience with God. When Paul wrote the believers in Philadelphia, he admonished them to work out their salvation with fear and trembling. (Philippians 2:12) New converts should also find a church home where the unadulterated word of God is being preached. God will also send Seasoned Believers who are worthy mentors to hold new converts accountable.

Living a Victorious Christian Life is not an easy journey. There will be challenges, victories and defeats. It is up to babes in Christ to seek out the truth in the Holy Bible. Gaining Biblical knowledge gives Christians the light they need along their journey. Thy word is a lamp unto my feet and light unto my path. (Psalm 119:105) Prayer is also an essential part of the Victorious Christian Life. According to 1 Thessalonians 5:17, we are to pray without ceasing. God also wants us to seek him first before we make our decisions. Seek ye first the Kingdom of God and His Righteousness and all these things shall be added unto you. (Matthew 6:33)

New Believers will experience joy along their journey. The joy of the Lord is your strength. (Nehemiah 8:10) When we continue to focus on God and develop an intimate relationship with HIM we have strength to endure the experiences of this life. Jesus himself was able to endure

many things when he walked the earth. He encourages us
when He says "In this life you will have tribulation but be

encouraged I have overcome the world." (John 16:33)
When God sent His son to die on the cross for our sins He
sent the perfect sacrifice. Jesus is able to identify with our
infirmities. (Hebrews 4:15)

As new converts live the Christian Life they will continue
to grow spiritually. New believers will learn to depend on
God when they develop an intimate relationship with HIM.
They will also learn to depend on the Holy Bible to cross
reference information to verify truth. God knows the
Christian journey is not easy. He knows that we have an
adversary who plots our demise. Stumbling blocks in this
world are inevitable. (Matthew 18:7) God wants us to
succeed and make it to the end of our journey. He works
through people to accomplish HIS will. He will send
Seasoned Believers to help along the way. Be encouraged as
you live a Victorious Christian Life. You will grow into a
Seasoned Believer who adds salt and light to help others in
dark places.

About The Author

About The Author

Brenda Diann Johnson was born in Dallas, Texas on September 14, 1970 to Robert Johnson and Thelma Byrd. She is the oldest of five children. She has a brother, sister, and two half brothers.

Brenda received her education from the Dallas and Wharton, Texas school systems. She graduated from Government, Law, and Law Enforcement Magnet High School in Dallas. She also received her Bachelor of Arts degree in Communications (Broadcast News) from UTA in Arlington, Texas and her Masters of Education Degree from Strayer University. She has her Texas license in Life, Health, Accident & HMO insurance, her Texas Adjusters License in All Lines, and she is a Texas Notary Public.

Today, Brenda is the CEO/Founder of The Young Scholar's Book Club which is a non-profit organization, ASWIFTT PUBLISHING, LLC which is the parent company of ASWIFTT Radio, The ASWIFTT Journal, ASWIFTT Television and ASWIFTT Records. She is also an experienced educator who has taught and tutored Pre-K through College. Brenda is the Dean of Education, Curriculum & Instruction for Best Practices Training Institute (B.P.T.I). She has also authored books and articles.

From 2001 to 2002, Brenda served as the chairperson for an entrepreneur group called STEP (Sowing Toward Everlasting Prosperity) and as the Potter's House Center Leader for the Plan Fund.

Brenda has served as a Sunday school teacher since age 18. She has faithfully served at Tabernacle Missionary Baptist Church, Oak Cliff Bible Fellowship, Rising Star Missionary Baptist Church and The Potter's House. She is currently a member of Prestonwood Baptist Church. In the community, she has served as a volunteer to organizations that help AIDS, HIV, and Syphilis patients.

Brenda currently lives in the Dallas/Fort Worth area with her family.

Services and Books

ASWIFTT PUBLISHING, LLC

Business advertising for Print & Media
BOOK PUBLISHING
ASWIFTT RADIO
ASWIFTT T.V.
THE ASWIFTT JOURNAL Newspaper

We have affordable advertising packages in our media categories. Some Ads are as low as $35.00. Email to ask about our Business Ads and Commercials.

You can visit us online or e-mail us:
www.aswifttpublishing.com
aswifttbookpublishing@yahoo.com

ASWIFTT RADIO
THE ASWIFTT JOURNAL
ASWIFTT TELEVISION

(Ambassadors Sent With Information For This Time) All three (3) mediums focus on delivering timely, newsworthy and accurate news stories. They also report on local, regional, national and international topics. For more information on ASWIFTT Radio, The ASWIFTT Journal and ASWIFTT Television visit the parent company ASWIFTT Publishing, LLC at www.aswifttpublishing.com.

The Young Scholar's Workbook:
Book I Vol. I (www.tysbookclub.org)

The Young Scholar's
Workbook: Book I Vol. I

By Brenda Diann Johnson

This is a fundraiser
publication for The Young
Scholar's Book Club. 50%
of the proceeds go to help
keep mentoring and tutoring
services free to students.
$19.95 plus s/h

How Did I Get Into This Mess?
You Compromised, Saith the Lord
2nd Edition

How Did I Get Into
This Mess? You
Compromised, Saith
the Lord 2nd Edition by

Brenda Diann Johnson

$12.95 plus s/h

Articles for Personal Growth and Development: Volume I

Articles for Personal Growth and Development: Vol. I by

Brenda Diann Johnson

$9.95 plus s/h

My Baby Sister

My Baby Sister by

Brenda Diann Johnson

$15.95 plus s/h

Available in English and Spanish

Advertise in an upcoming

ASWIFTT PUBLISHING, LLC Book

Your business will have a permanent advertising spot in An ASWIFTT PUBLISHING, LLC Book. The book that carries your Business Ad will continue to advertise your business every time the book is printed and purchased by a customer. For more information on ASWIFTT PUBLISHING, LLC book advertising email us at: aswifttbookpublishing@yahoo.com

How Did I Get Into This Mess?

You Compromised Saith the Lord

Brenda Diann Johnson

$35.00 Business Ad

Includes:

1. Business Name
2. Address

$100.00 Business Ad

Includes:

1. Logo
2. Business Name
3. Address
4. Phone Number
5. Website
6. Short Bio

$65.00 Business Ad

Includes:

1. Logo
2. Business Name
3. Address
4. Phone Number
5. Website

ASWIFTT PUBLISHING, LLC ORDER FORM

Name_____

Address_____

City_____

State_____

Zip_____
Item _____Amount_____
Item _____Amount_____
Item _____Amount_____

Add $8.50 for Shipping and Handling on books
Total:_____

Make Checks, Money Orders, Cashier's Checks out to:

ASWIFTT PUBLISHING, LLC

P.O. Box 380669

Duncanville, Texas 75138

Credit Card Orders:
Circle One: Master Card   Visa   American Express
Discover
Credit Card Number_____
Exp. Date_____
Three Digit Security Number on back of
Card_____

Name & Address Associated with Credit Card:

Authorization Signature_____**Date**_____

Your order will be processed or shipped 2 to 4 weeks from the date order is received. Direct concerns on orders email: aswifttbookpublishing@yahoo.com

Thank you for your business! Make copies of this form.